GRIEG

HOLBERG SUITE
Op. 40

Edited by
Richard W. Sargeant, Jr.

Study Score
Partitur

SERENISSIMA MUSIC, INC.

CONTENTS

1. Praeludium 3

2. Sarabande 18

3. Air 25

4. Gavotte 39

5. Rigaudon 49

ORCHESTRA

Violins I
Violins II
Violas
Violoncellos
Double Basses

Duration: ca. 20 minutes

First performance: March, 1885
Bergen, Norway
String Orchestra
Edvard Grieg, conductor

ISBN: 978-1-60874-152-6
This score is a newly reserached and engraved edition
prepared by the editor published for the first time.

Printed in the USA
First Printing: June, 2015

HOLBERG SUITE
Op. 40
1. Preludium

Edvard Grieg
Edited by Richard W. Sargeant, Jr.

4

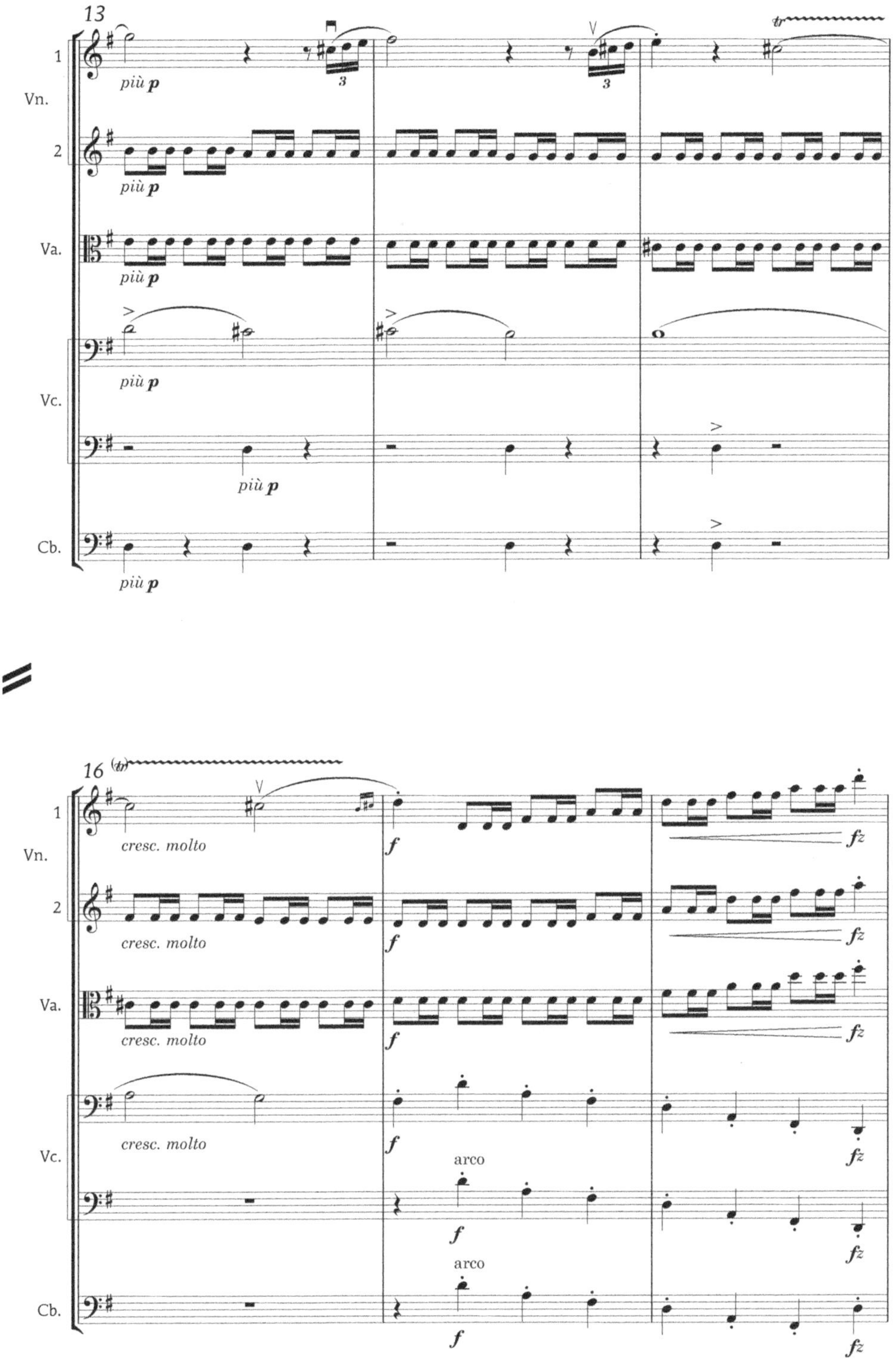
13
Vn. 1
Vn. 2
Va.
Vc.
Cb.
più p
tr
16
cresc. molto
f
fz
arco

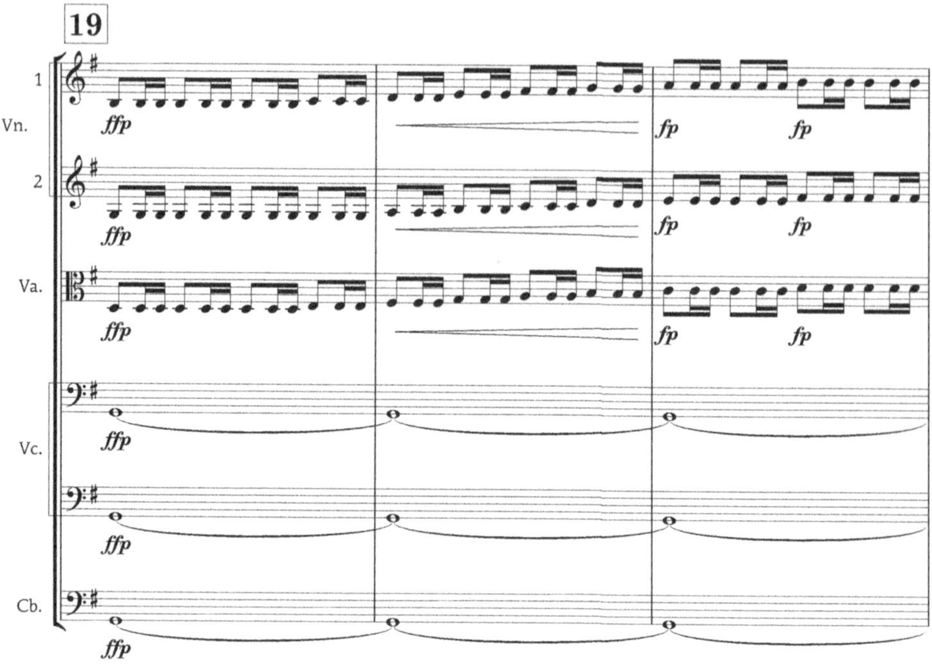
19
Vn. 1
Vn. 2
Va.
Vc.
Cb.
ffp
fp

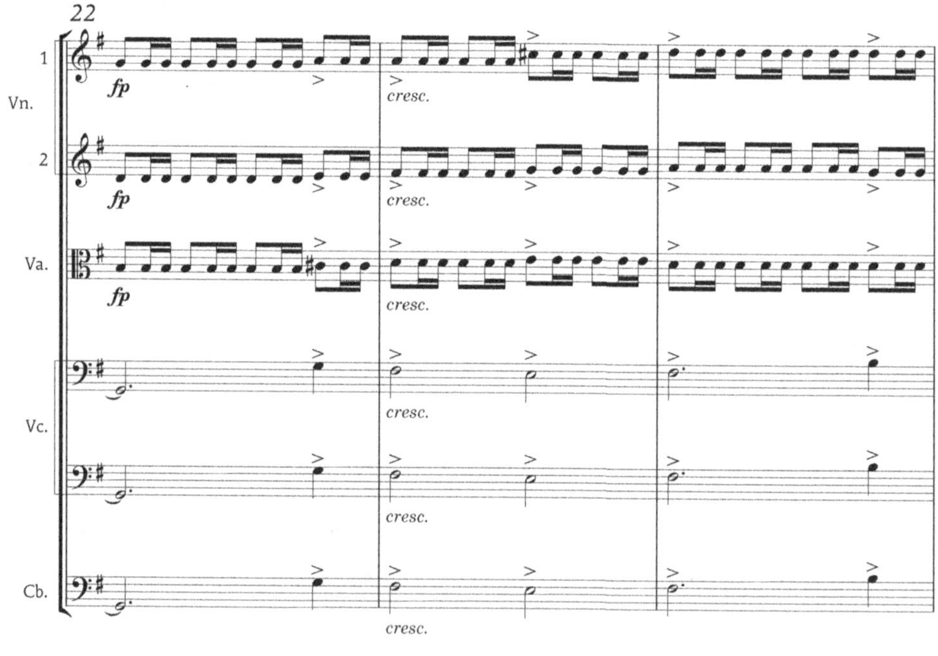
22
Vn. 1
Vn. 2
Va.
Vc.
Cb.
fp
cresc.

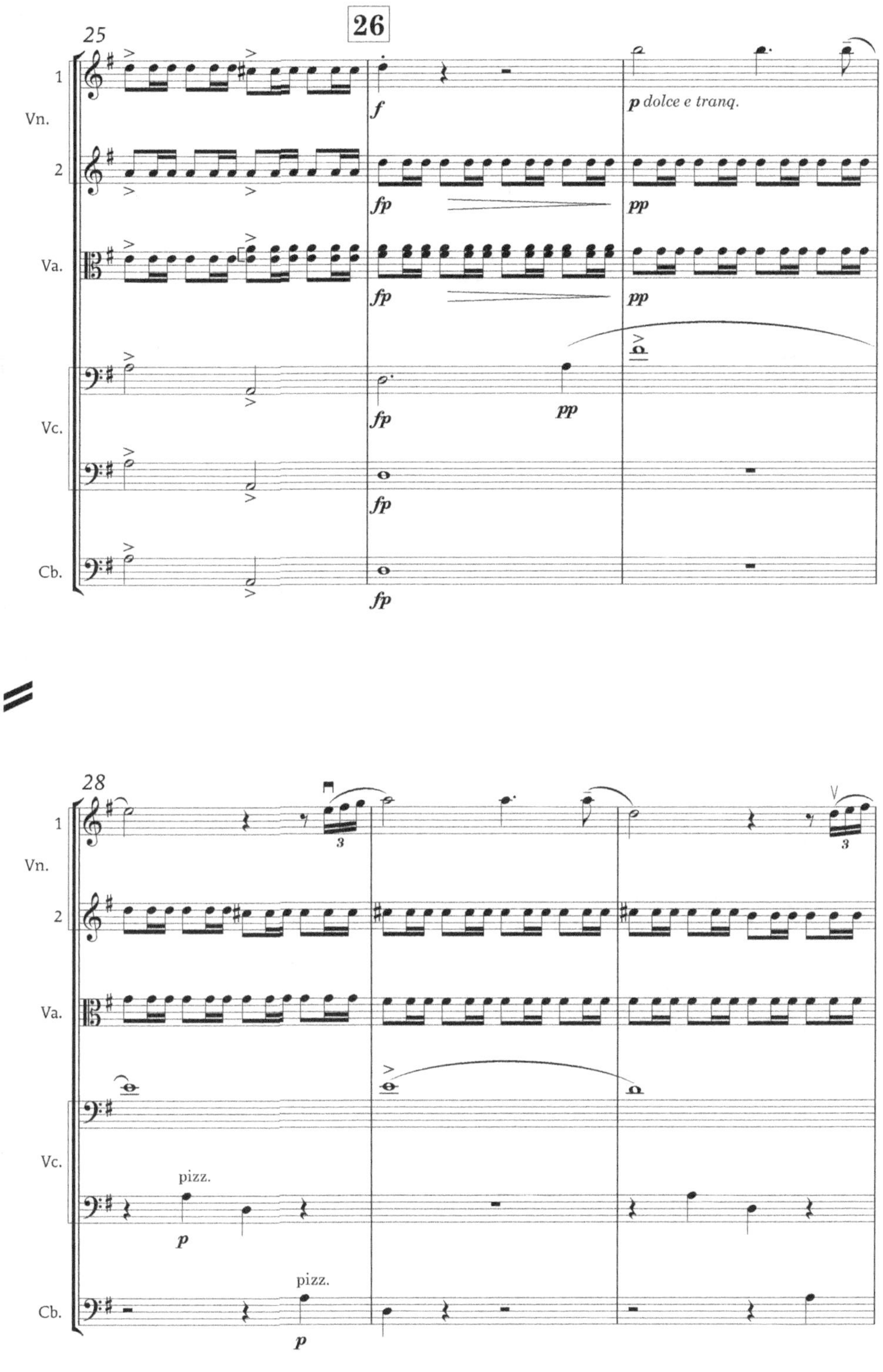
25
26
Vn.
1
2
Va.
Vc.
Cb.
f
p dolce e tranq.
fp
pp
28
3
pizz.
p

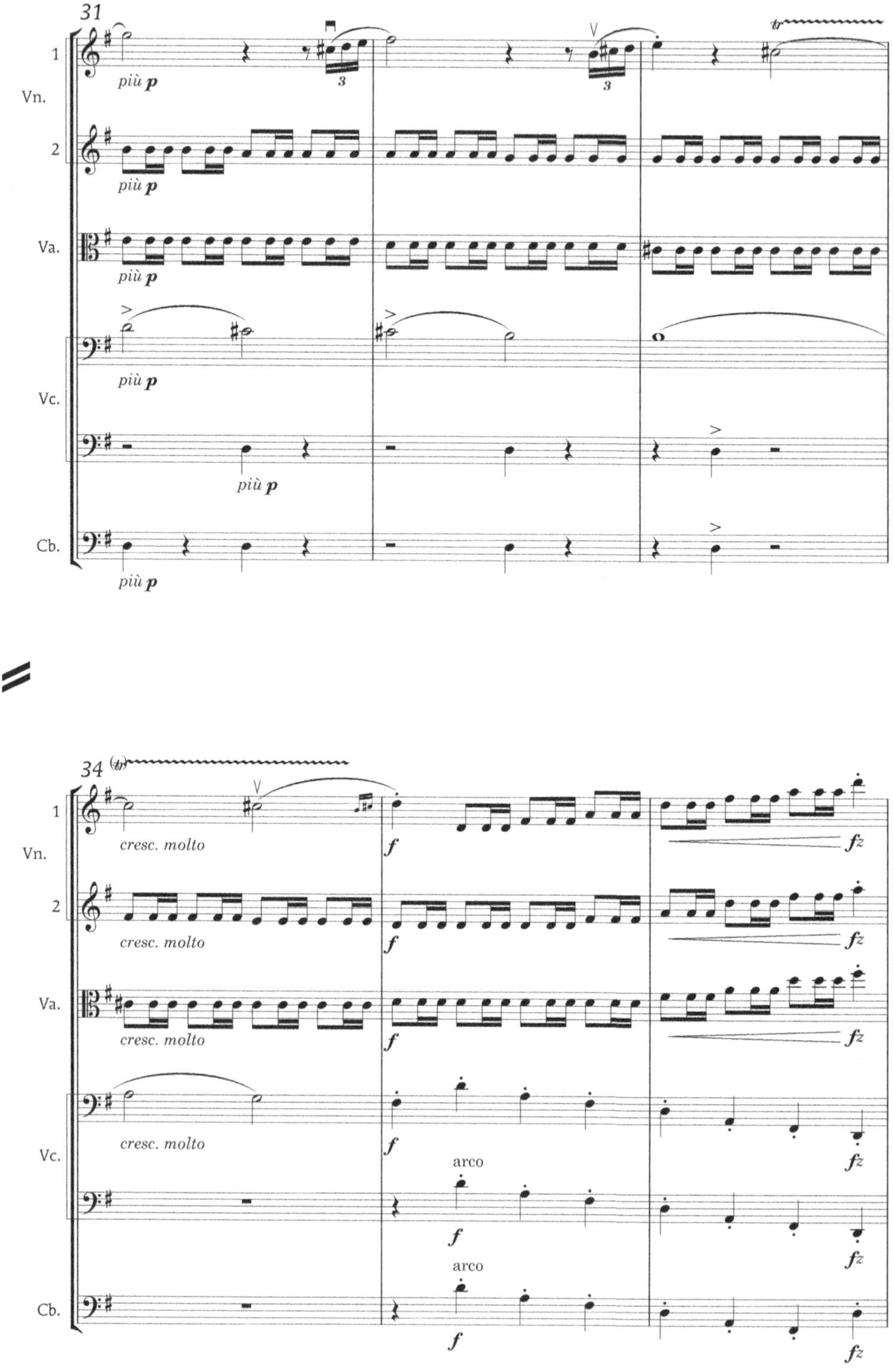
31
Vn.
1
2
Va.
Vc.
Cb.
più p
34
cresc. molto
arco

9

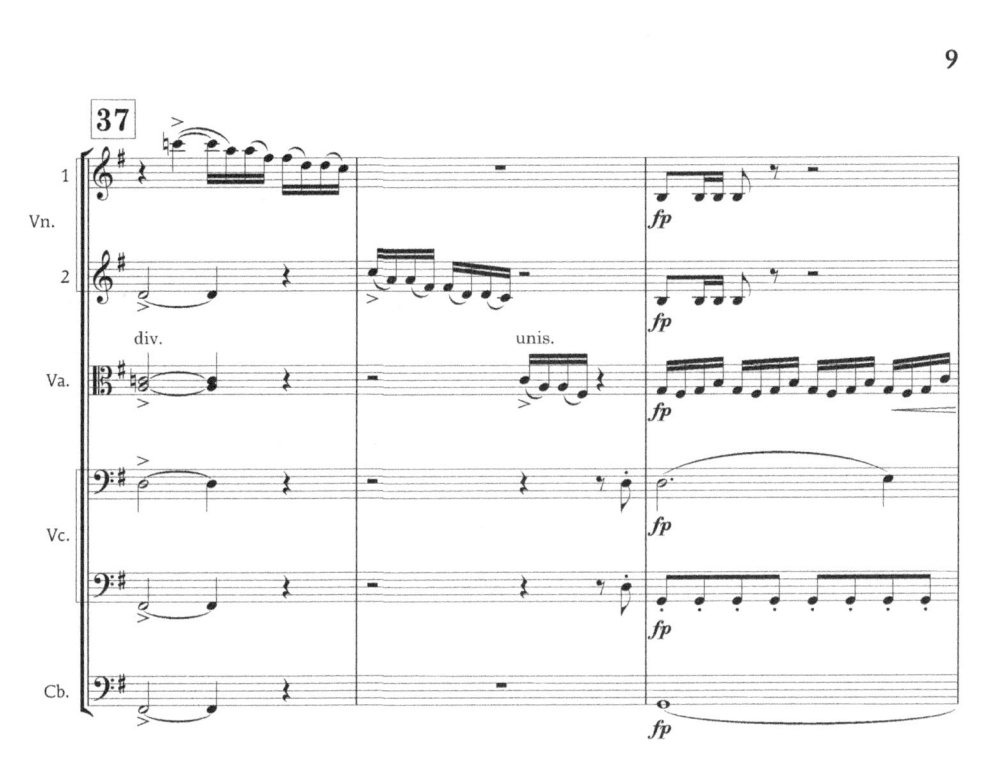

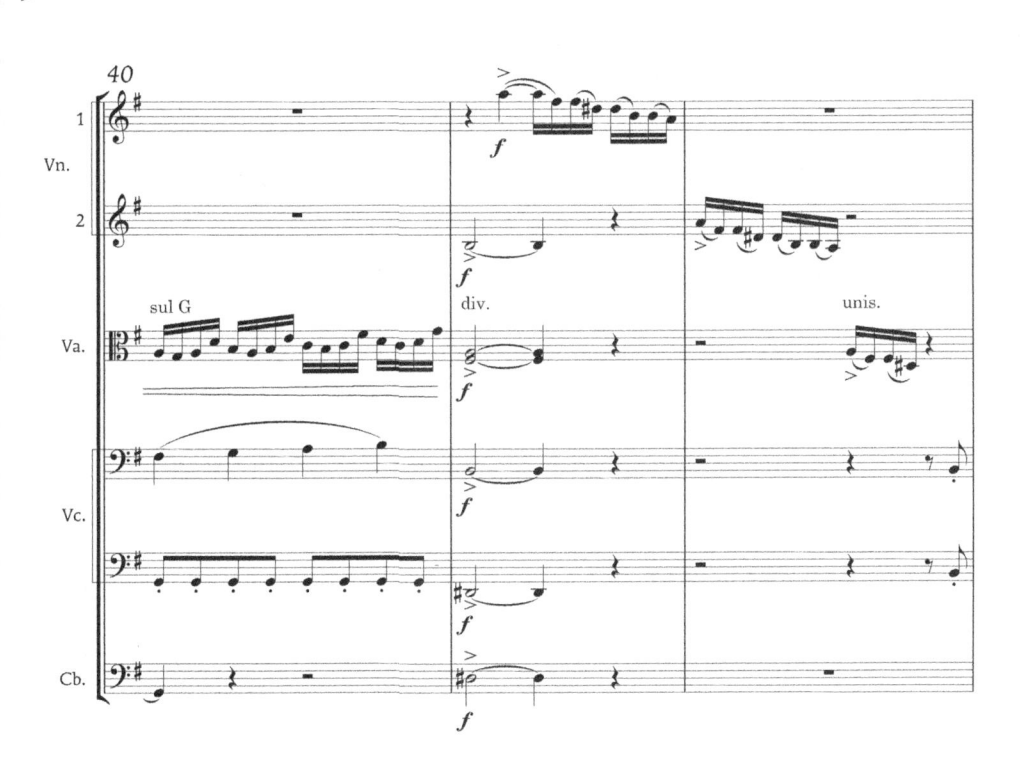

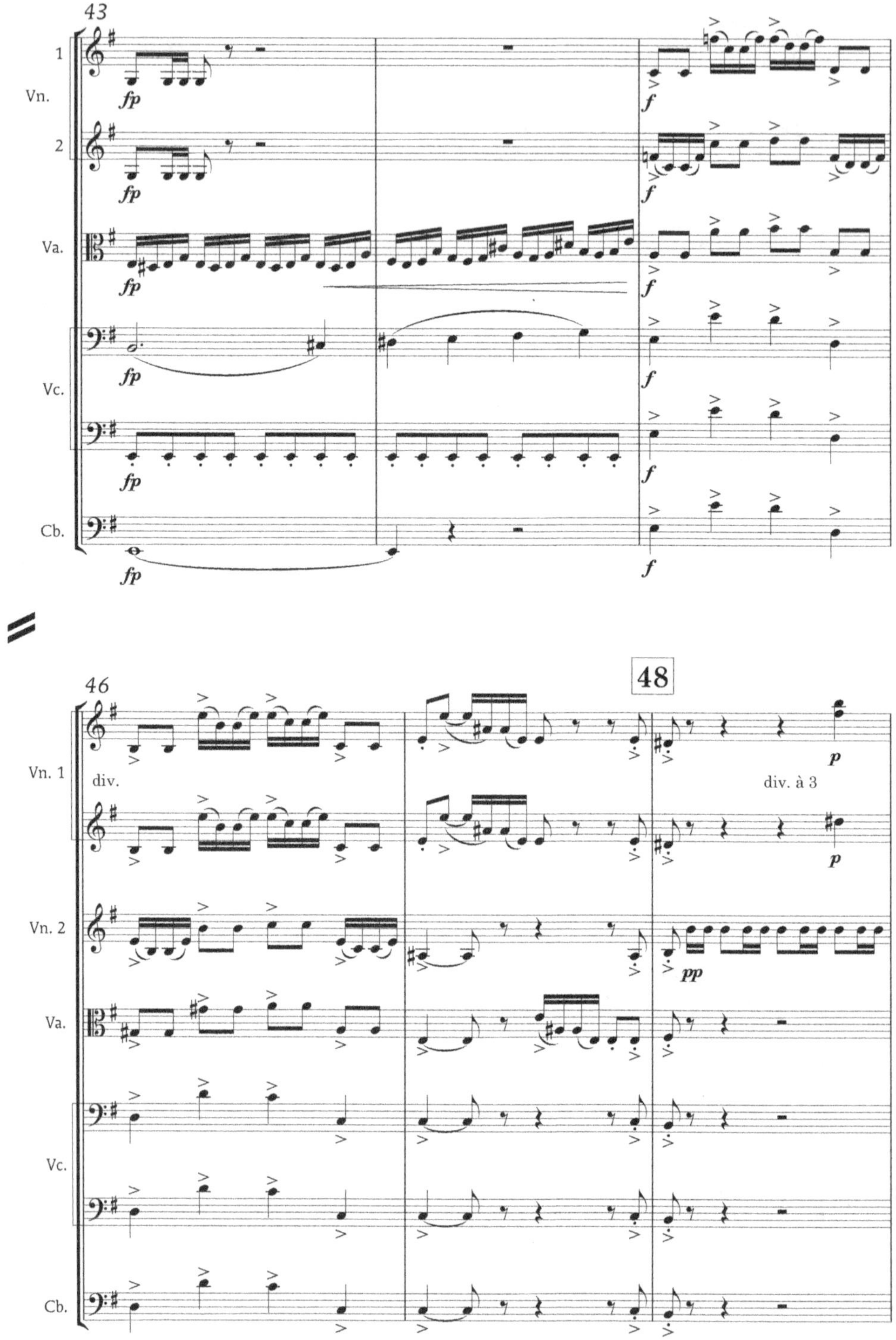
43
Vn. 1
2
Va.
Vc.
Cb.
fp
f
46
48
Vn. 1
div.
div. à 3
p
Vn. 2
pp
Va.
Vc.
Cb.

49
Vn. 1
Vn. 2
pizz.
Va.
p
Vc.
Cb.
52
più p
Vn. 1
più p
Vn. 2
più p
Va.
2 soli pizz.
Vc.
pp
Cb.

55
Vn. 1
pp
pp
Vn. 2
div.
pp
cresc. molto
Va.
arco div.
pp
cresc. molto
Vc.
pp
Cb.
58
Vn. 1
f
fz
div. à 2
f
fz
Vn. 2
f
fz
unis.
Va.
f
fz
unis.
Vc.
arco
f
fz
4 soli
arco
f
fz
Cb.
f
fz

13

14

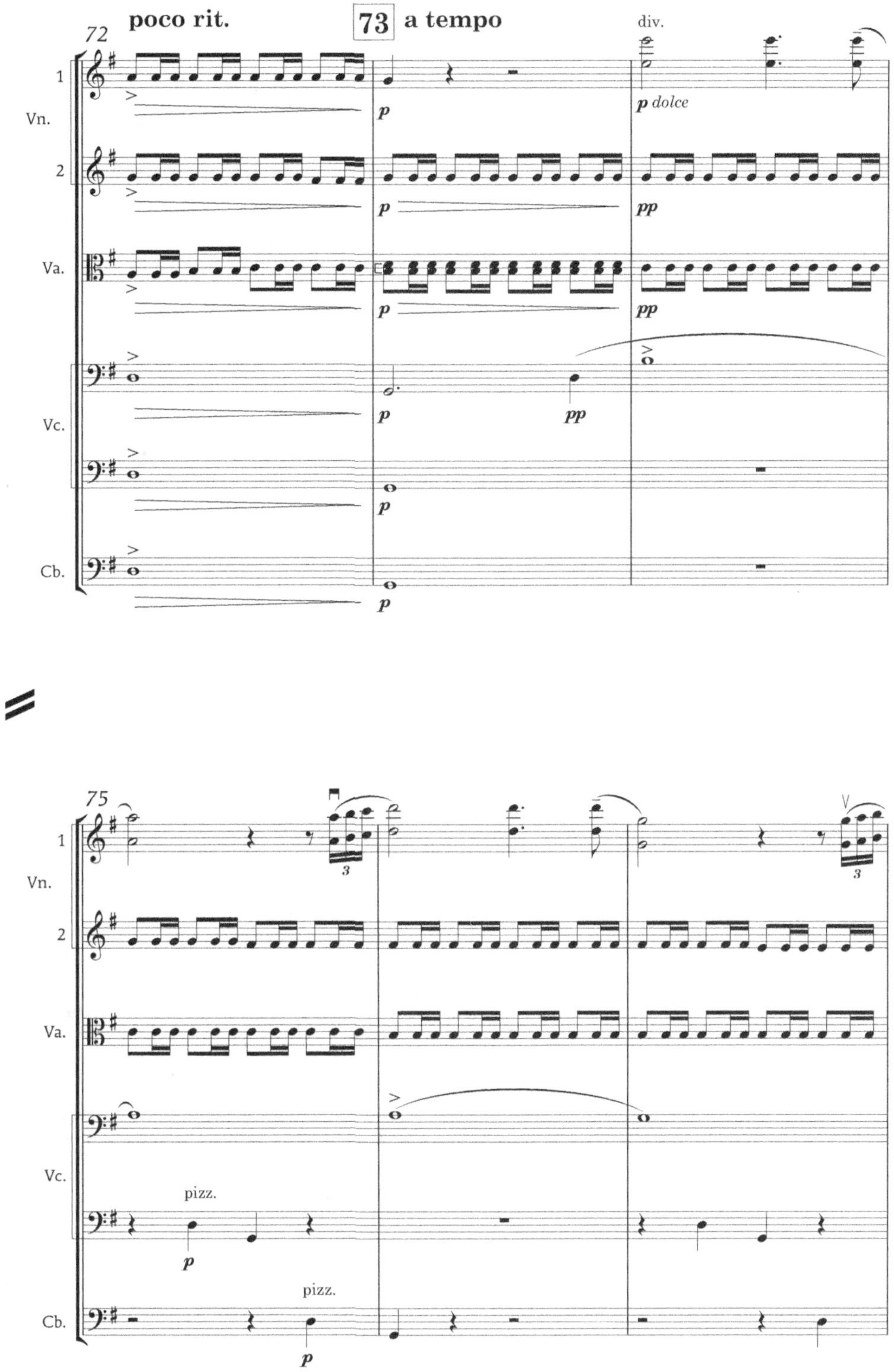
72
poco rit.
73
a tempo
div.
Vn.
1
2
Va.
Vc.
Cb.
p dolce
p
pp
75
pizz.

78
Vn.
1
2
Va.
Vc.
Cb.
più p
tr
3

82
81
(tr)
Vn.
1
2
Va.
Vc.
Cb.
cresc. molto
unis.
arco
f
fz

17

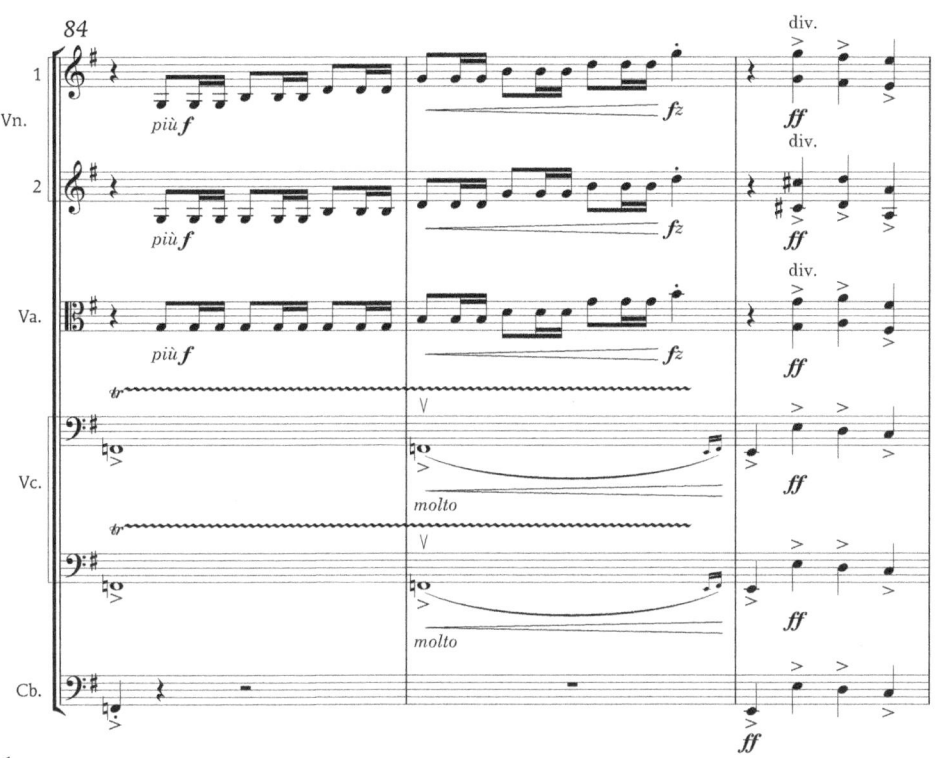

2. Sarabande

19

20
sul G
Vn.
1
2
unis.
unis.
Va.
solo
tutti
Vc.
Cb.
p
mf
cresc.
24
25
3 soli
solo
pp
più pp

21

41 un poco mosso
39
sul D
Vn.
1
2
Va.
Vc.
Cb.
f
p
pizz.
43
solo
tutti
mf
cresc.

47
sul G
49
Vn.
1
2
mf
Va.
mf
Vc.
mf
pp
3 soli
mf
pp
solo
Cb.
pp
51
poco a poco rit.
div.
p
cresc.
div.
p
cresc.
div.
p
cresc.
più pp
tutti div.
più pp
più pp

57 Tempo I
56
Vn.
Va.
Vc.
Cb.
cresc.
tutti arco
60
unis.
sul D
sul G
cresc. molto

3. Gavotte

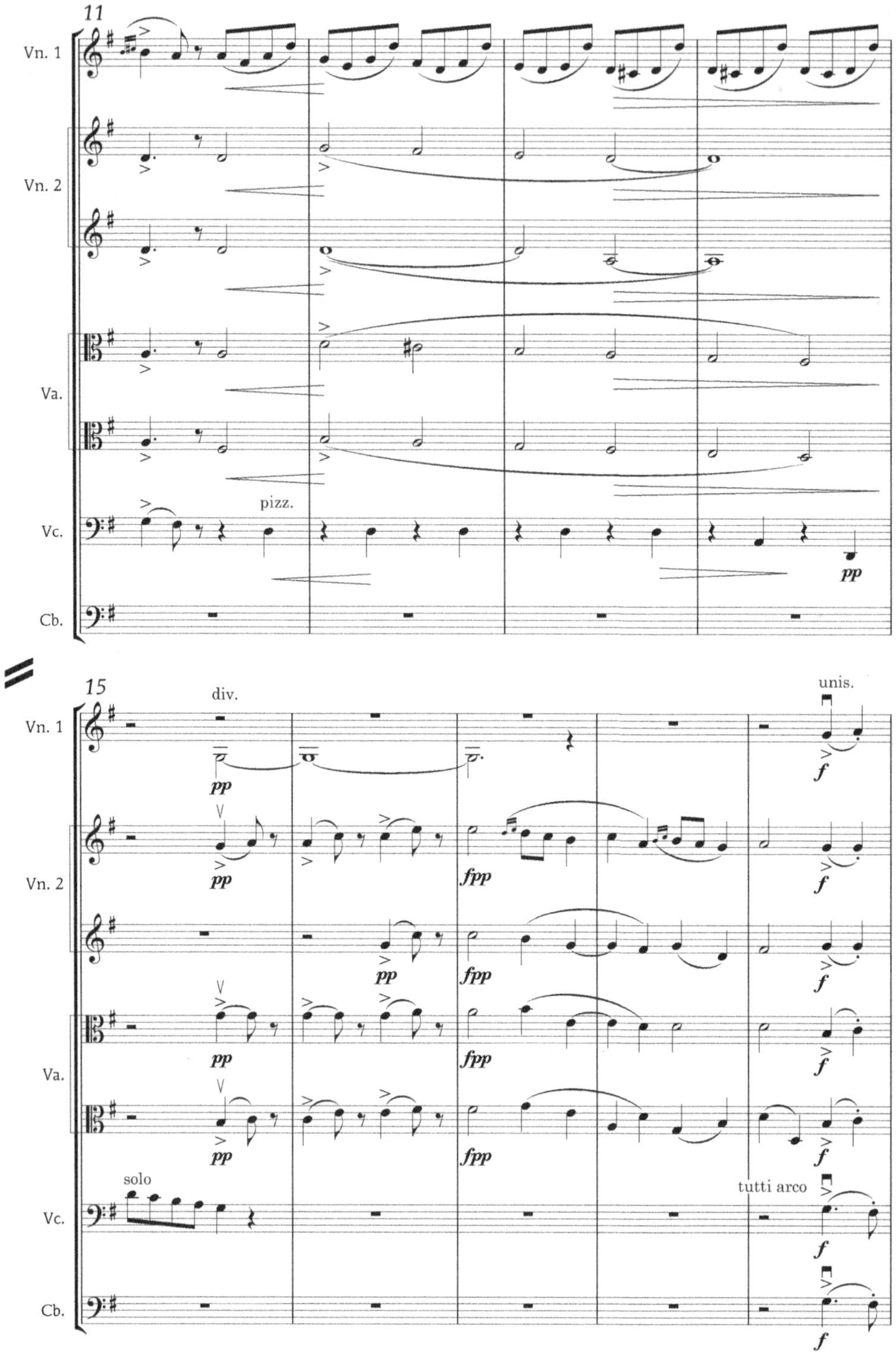
11
Vn. 1
Vn. 2
Va.
pizz.
Vc.
pp
Cb.
15
div.
unis.
pp
fpp
f
solo
tutti arco

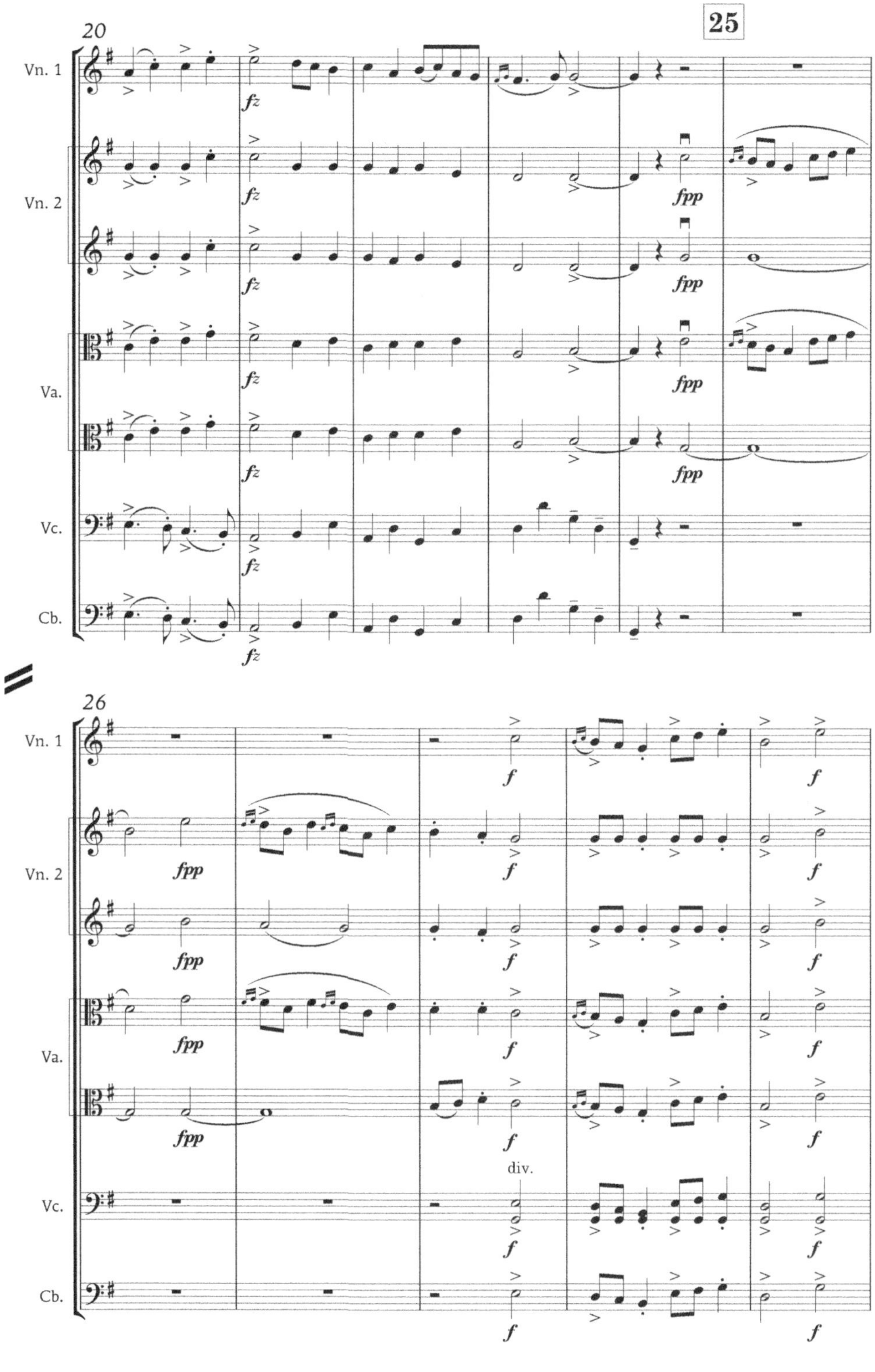
20
25
Vn. 1
Vn. 2
Va.
Vc.
Cb.
fz
fpp
26
f
div.

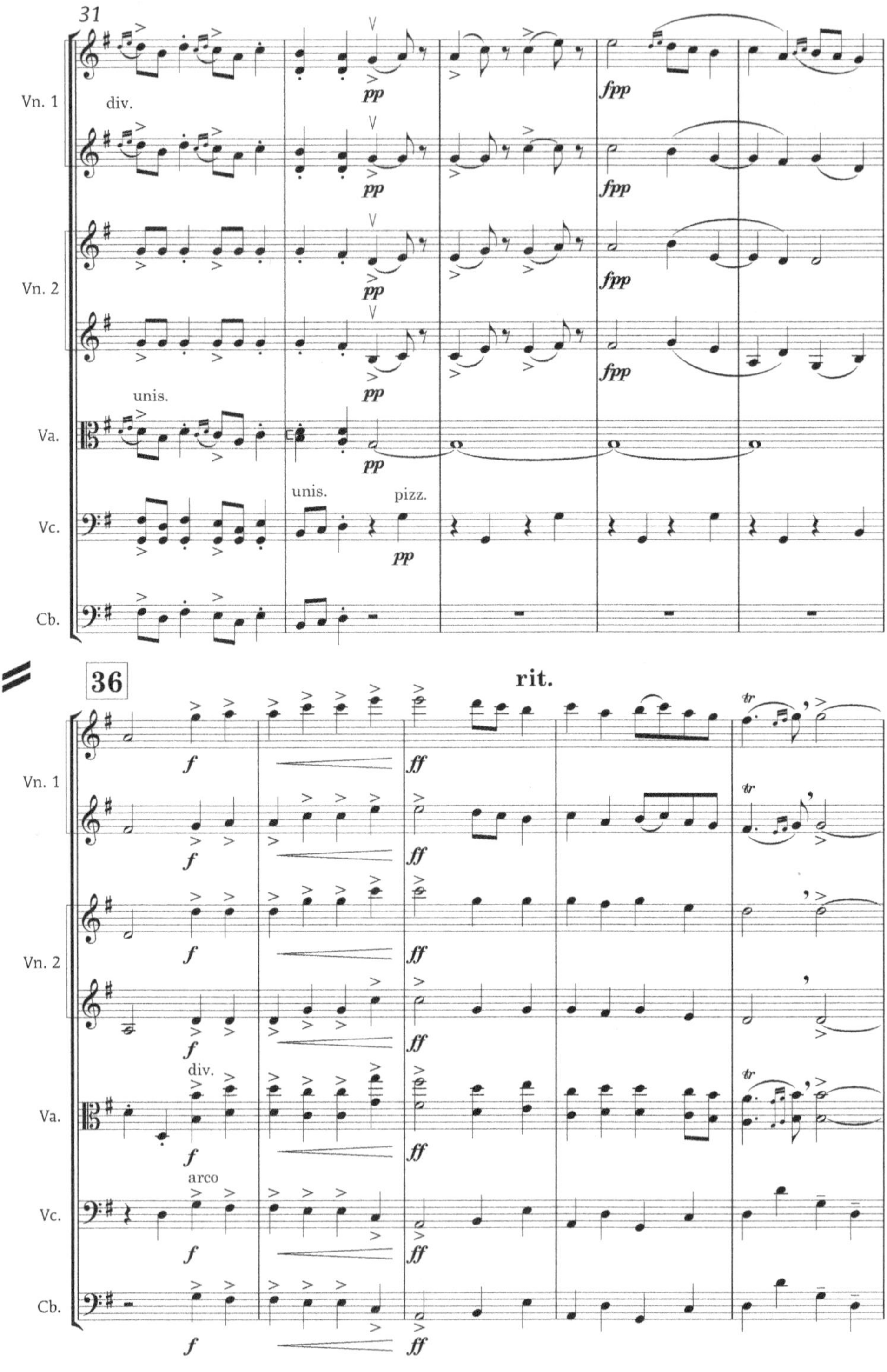
31
Vn. 1
div.
pp
fpp
Vn. 2
unis.
Va.
Vc.
pizz.
Cb.
36
rit.
f
ff
arco
tr

Musette
poco più mosso

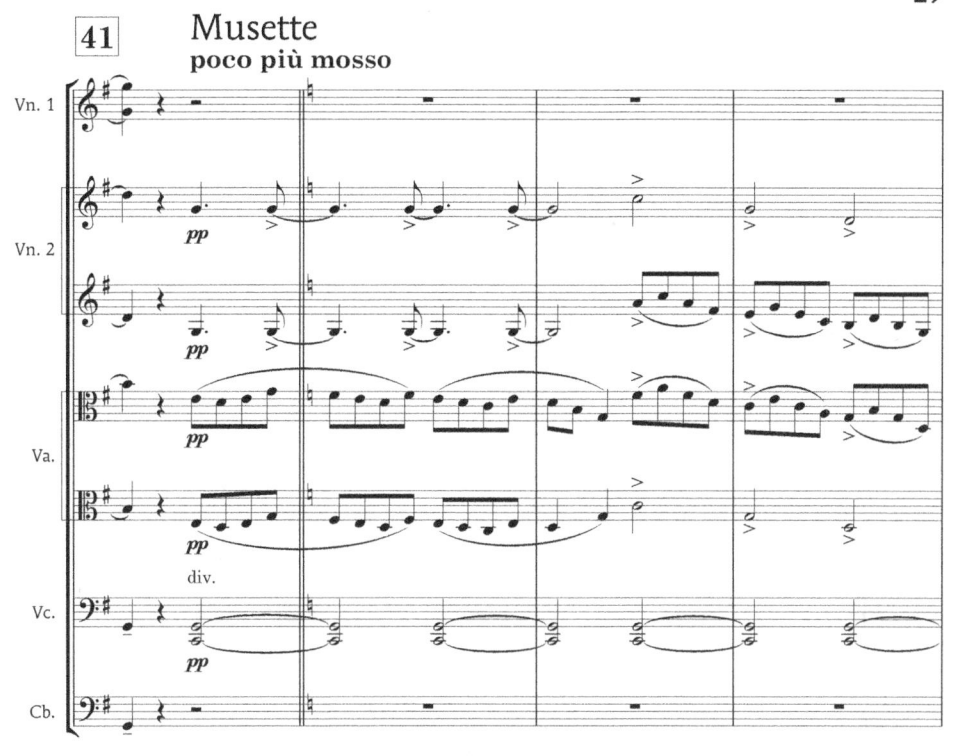

49
50
Vn. 1
Vn. 2
Va.
Vc.
Cb.
p
cresc.
cant.
unis.
p cant.
pizz.
unis. pizz.
54
f
arco

31

66
Vn. 1
Vn. 2
Va.
Vc.
Cb.
p
unis.
p cant.
unis.
pizz.
p
70
Vn. 1
Vn. 2
Va.
Vc.
Cb.
p
cresc.
cant.
cresc.
cant.
cresc.
p
cresc.
p
cresc.
pizz.
cresc.

33

82
Vn. 1
Vn. 2
Va.
Vc.
Cb.
pp
div. pizz.
pp
86
Tempo I
Vn. 1
Vn. 2
Va.
Vc.
Cb.
pp
pp
pp
pp

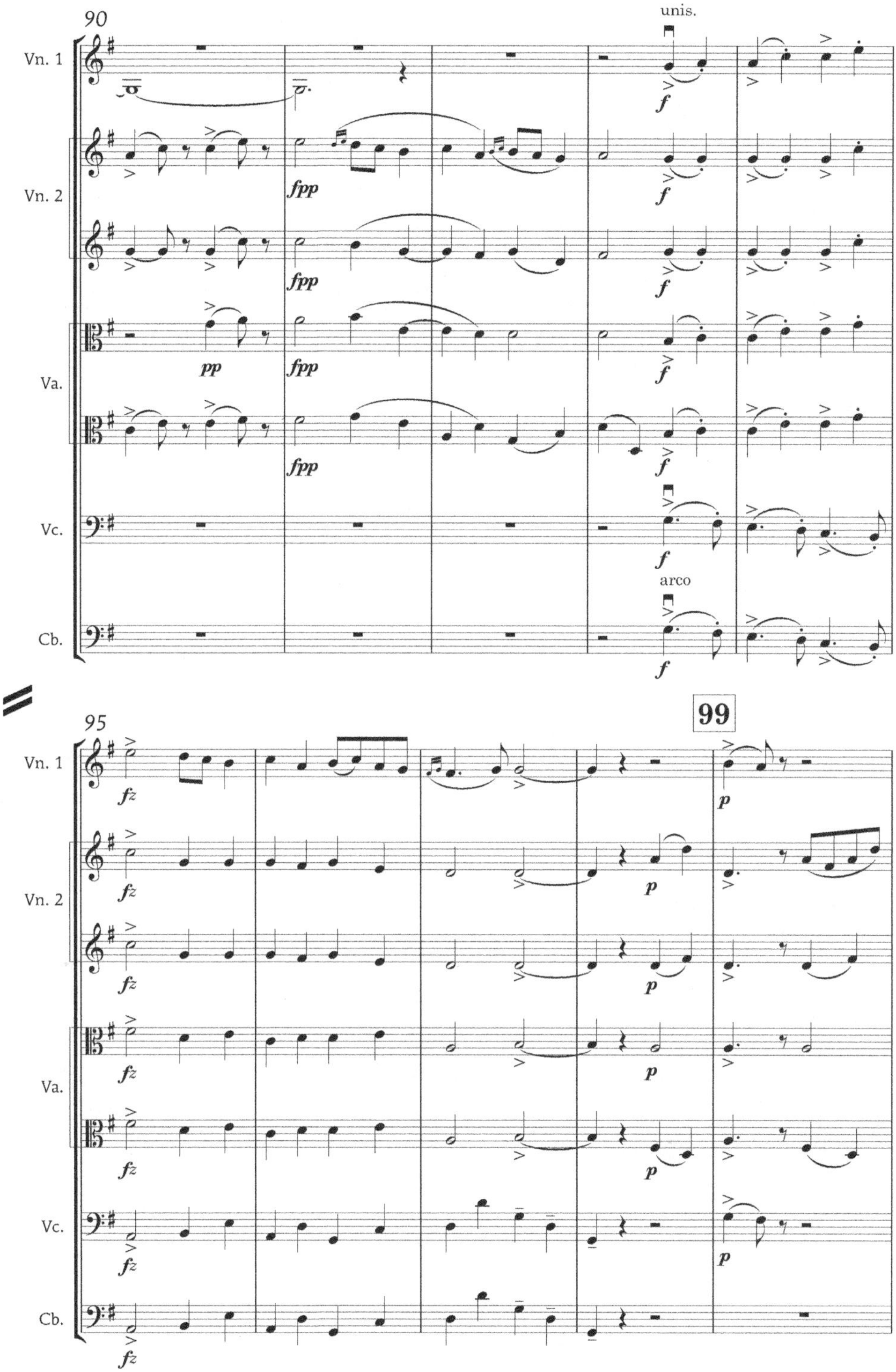
90
unis.
arco
Vn. 1
Vn. 2
Va.
Vc.
Cb.
pp
fpp
f
95
99
fz
p

36

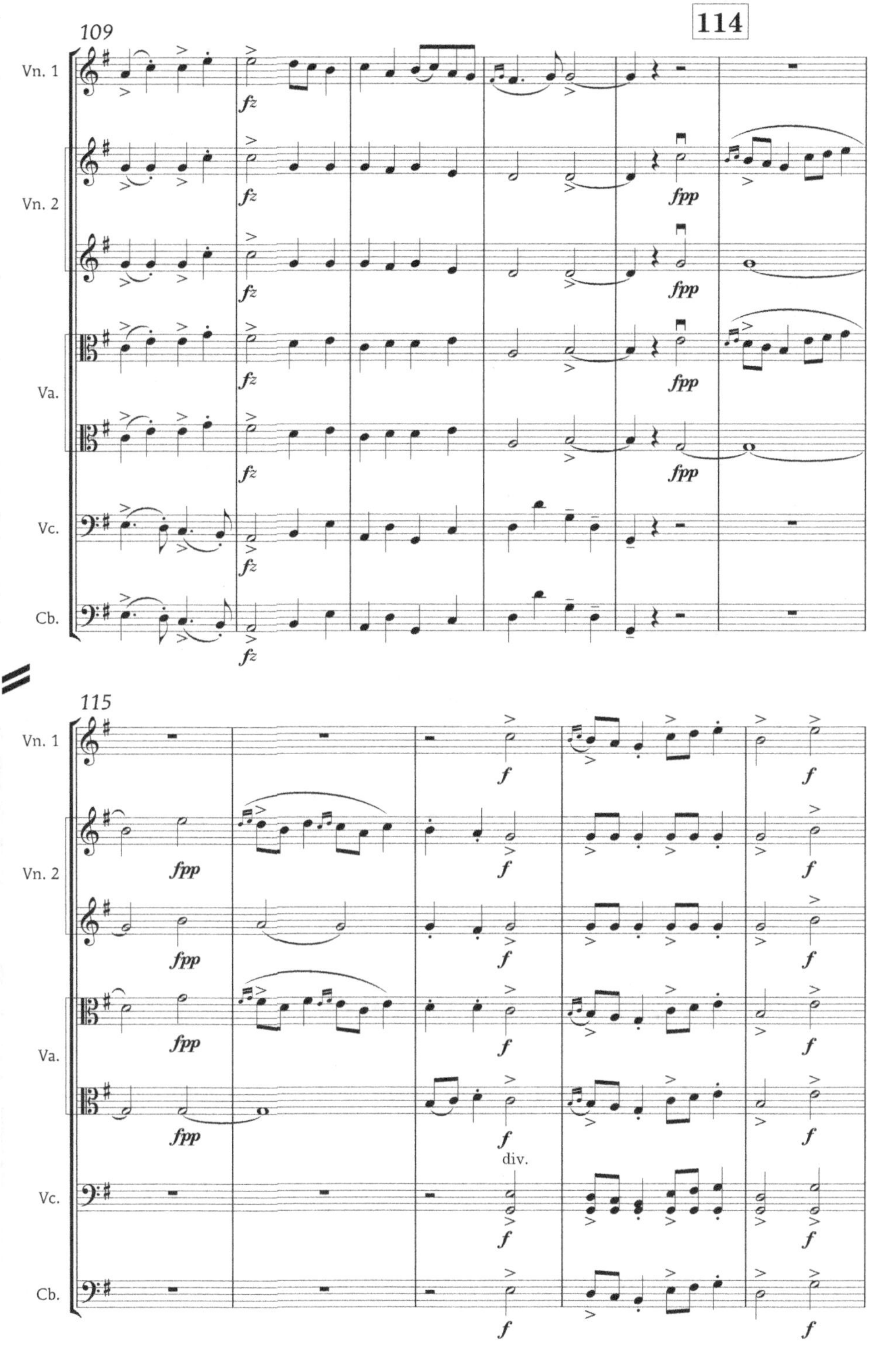
109
114
Vn. 1
Vn. 2
Va.
Vc.
Cb.
fz
fpp
115
f
div.

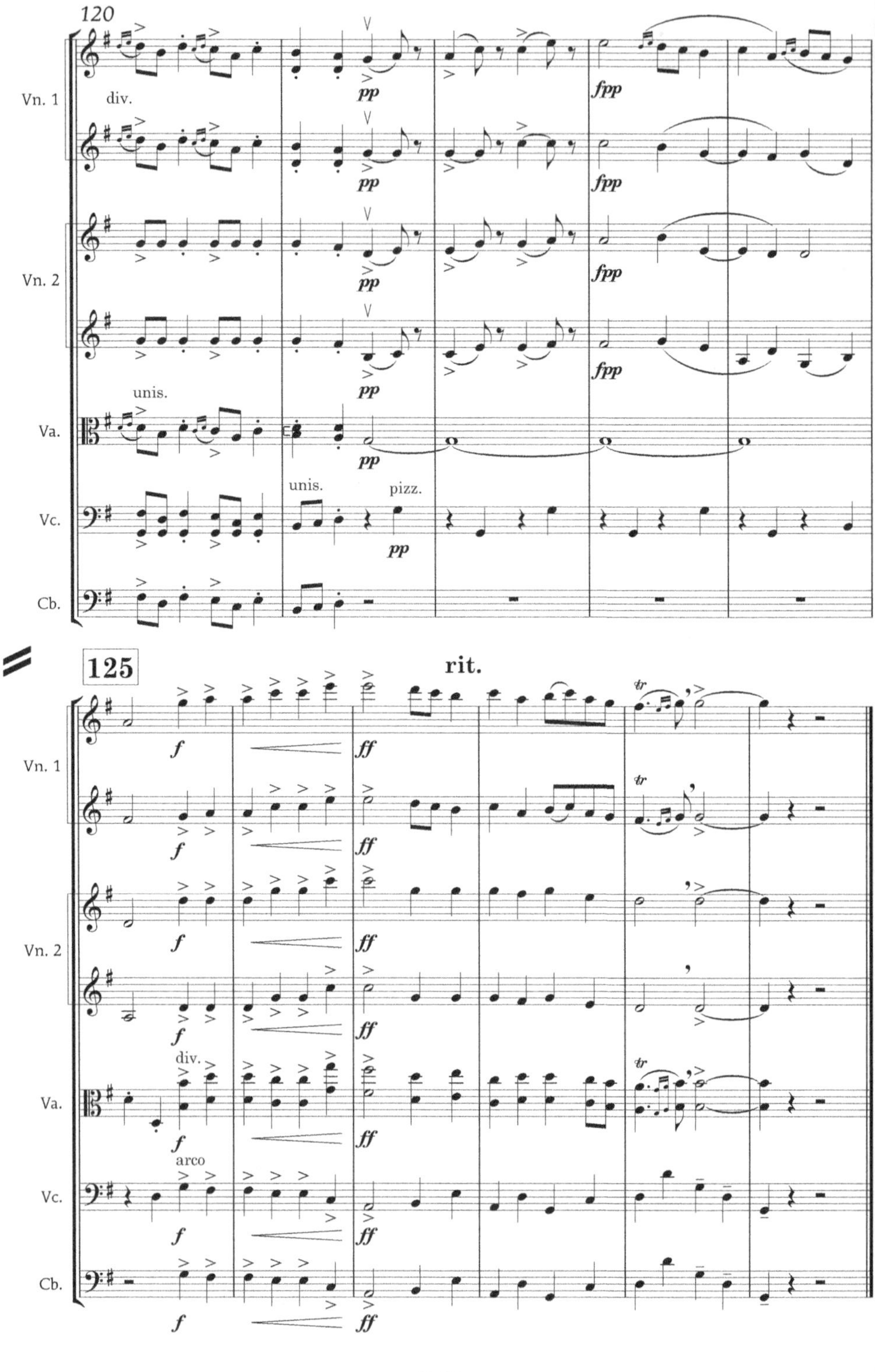
120
Vn. 1
div.
pp
fpp
Vn. 2
unis.
Va.
pizz.
Vc.
Cb.
125
rit.
f
ff
div.
arco

4. Air

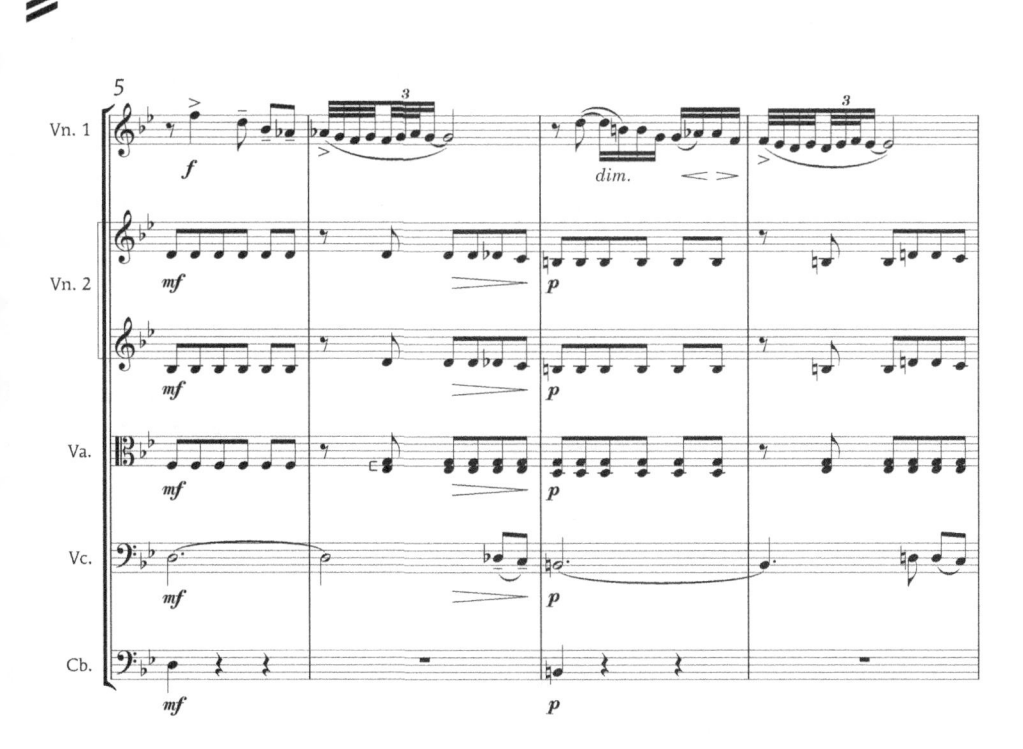

9
Vn. 1
Vn. 2
Va.
Vc.
Cb.
div.
p
cresc.
cant.
arco
13
rit.
molto rit.
16
a tempo
unis.
f
dim.
ffp
pp
pizz.
3

41

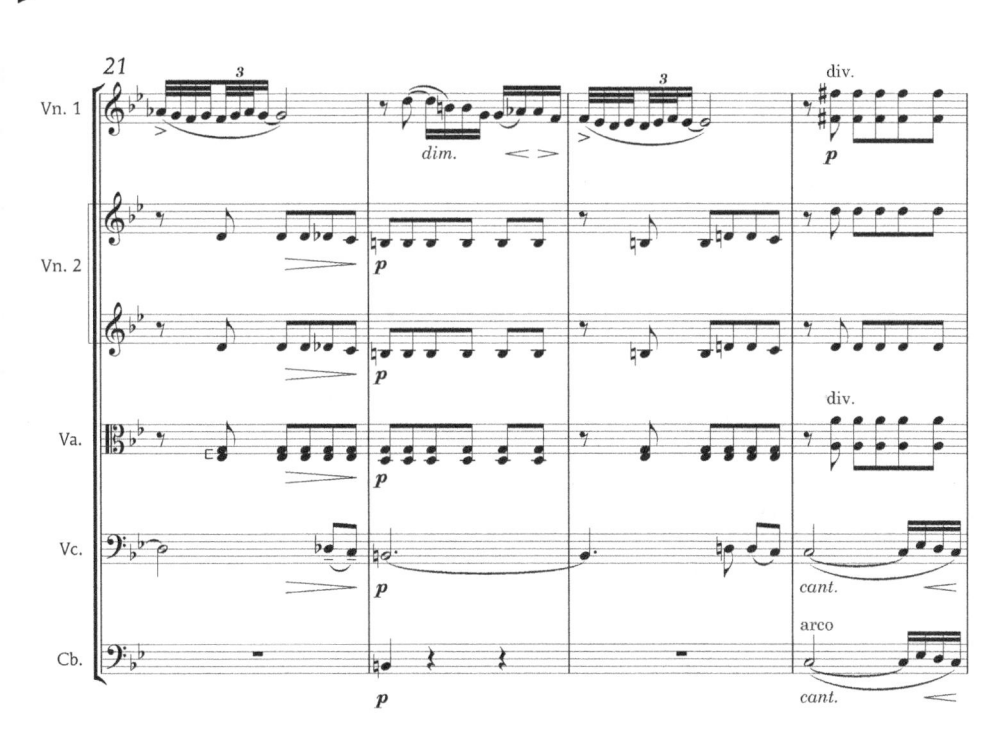

25
Vn. 1
Vn. 2
Va.
Vc.
Cb.
cresc.
f
dim.
div.
rit.
molto rit.
31 a tempo
29
unis.
ffp
pp
pizz.

43

poco rit.
40
div.
Vn.
1
2
Va.
Vc.
Cb.
ff
unis.
div.
arco
cresc.
44
a tempo
unis.
ffz
dim.
p
pizz.
arco

48
Vn. 1
2
Va.
Vc.
Cb.
3
unis.
cresc.
unis.
51
cresc.
dim.
div.
dim.
dim.
dim.
dim.
pizz.

poco rit.
55
a tempo
54
Vn.
1
2
Va.
Vc.
Cb.
pp
f cant.
molto
arco
div.
pizz.
3
57
Vn. 1
Vn. 2
mf
dim.
ff

47

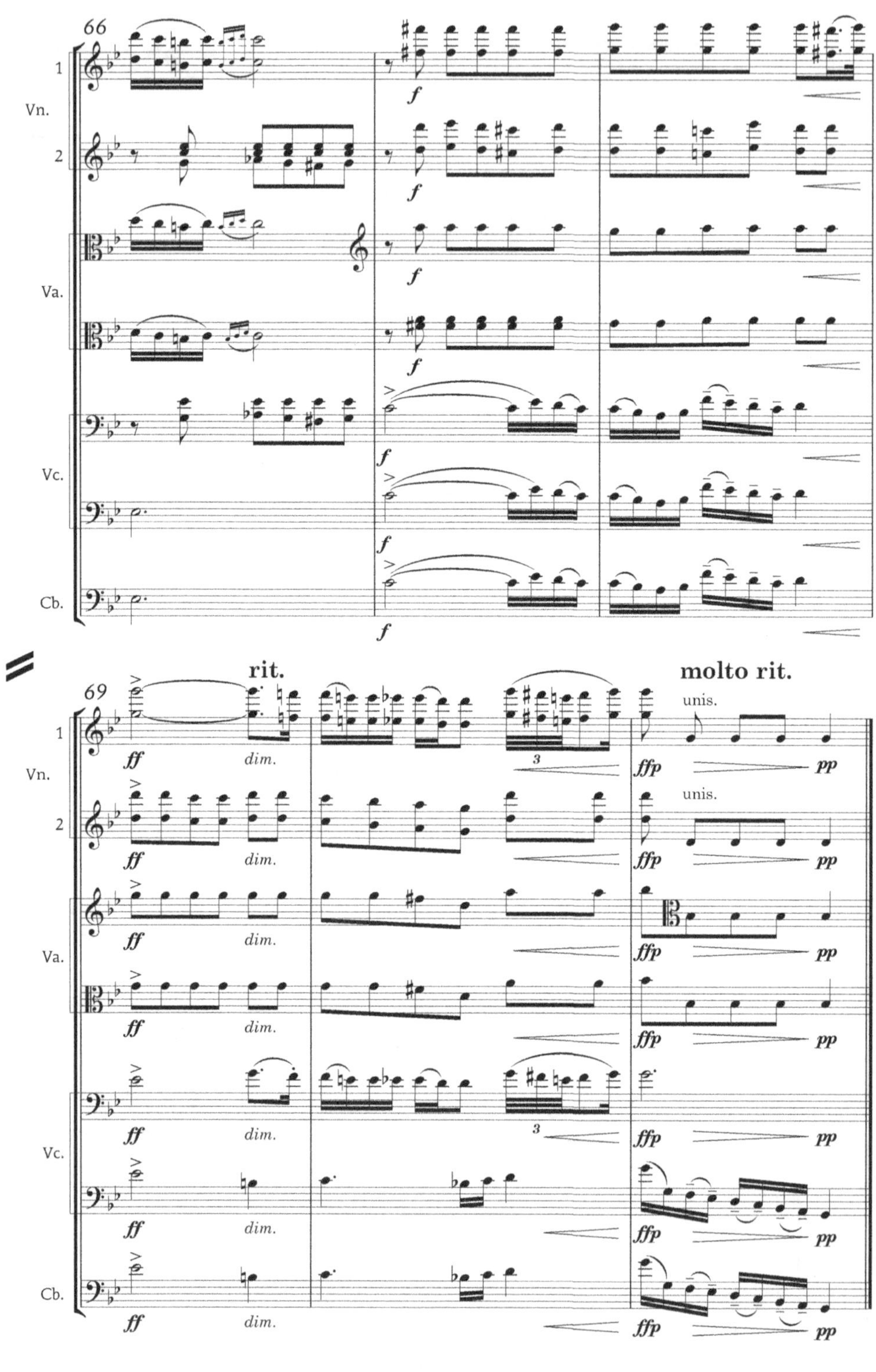
66
Vn.
1
2
Va.
Vc.
Cb.
f
69
rit.
molto rit.
unis.
ff
dim.
3
ffp
pp

5. Rigaudon

Allegro con brio ♩ = 144

9
Solo Vn.
fp
Vn.
1
2
pp
pp
Solo Va.
fp
pizz.
Va.
f
Vc.
Cb.
13
Solo Vn.
cresc.
f
p
Vn.
1
2
f
f
Solo Va.
f
arco
Va.
f
Vc.
f
Cb.
f

51

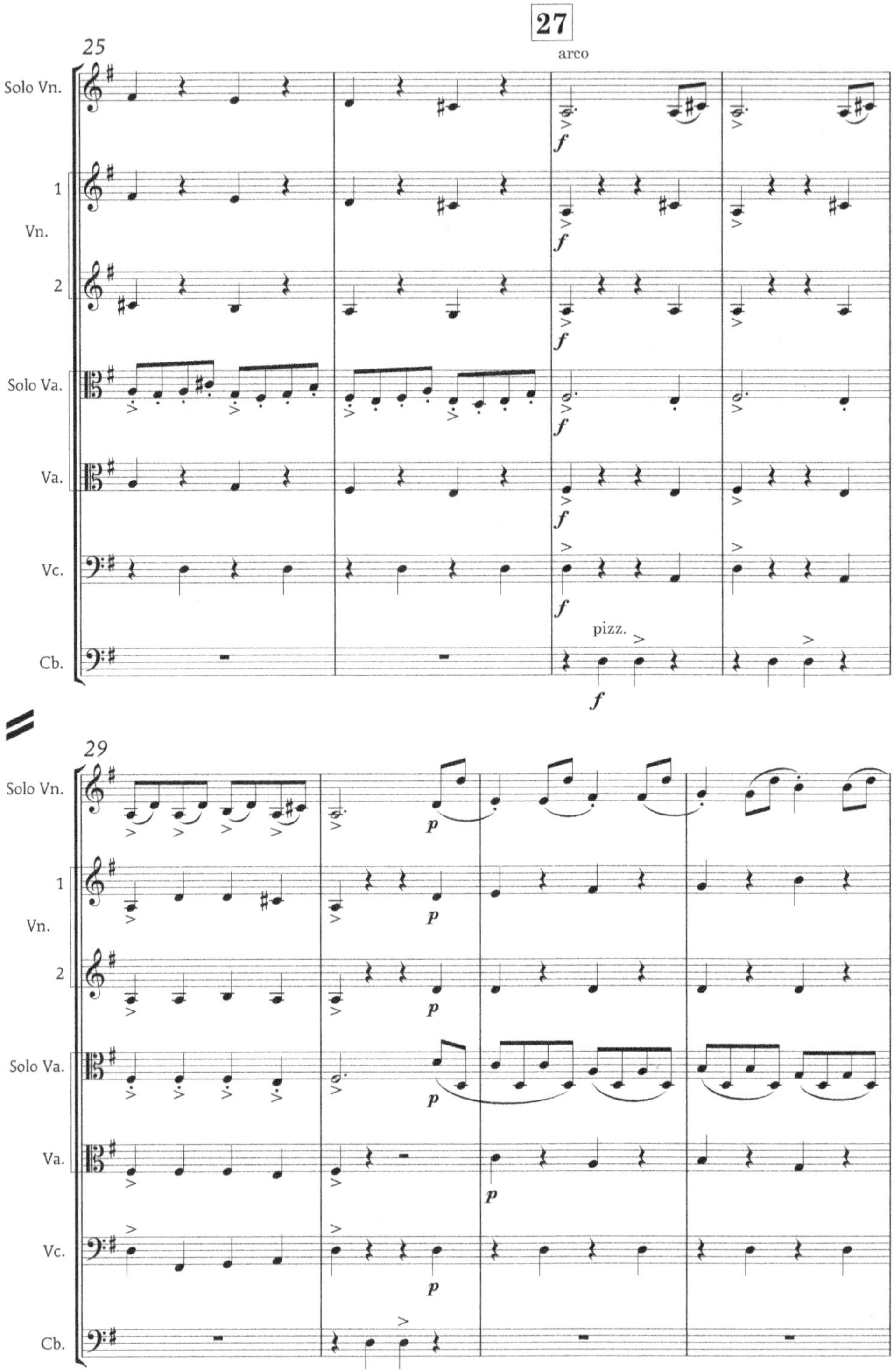
27
25
arco
Solo Vn.
1
Vn.
2
Solo Va.
Va.
Vc.
Cb.
f
pizz.
29
p

53

41
Solo Vn.
1
Vn.
2
Solo Va.
Va.
Vc.
Cb.
arco
ff
arco
ff
45
rit.
a tempo
unis. arco
unis. arco
arco
ff
ffz
p

49
Solo Vn.
unis.
Vn.
1
2
unis.
p
Solo Va.
pizz.
Va.
Vc.
Cb.
53
pizz.
cresc.
pizz.
p

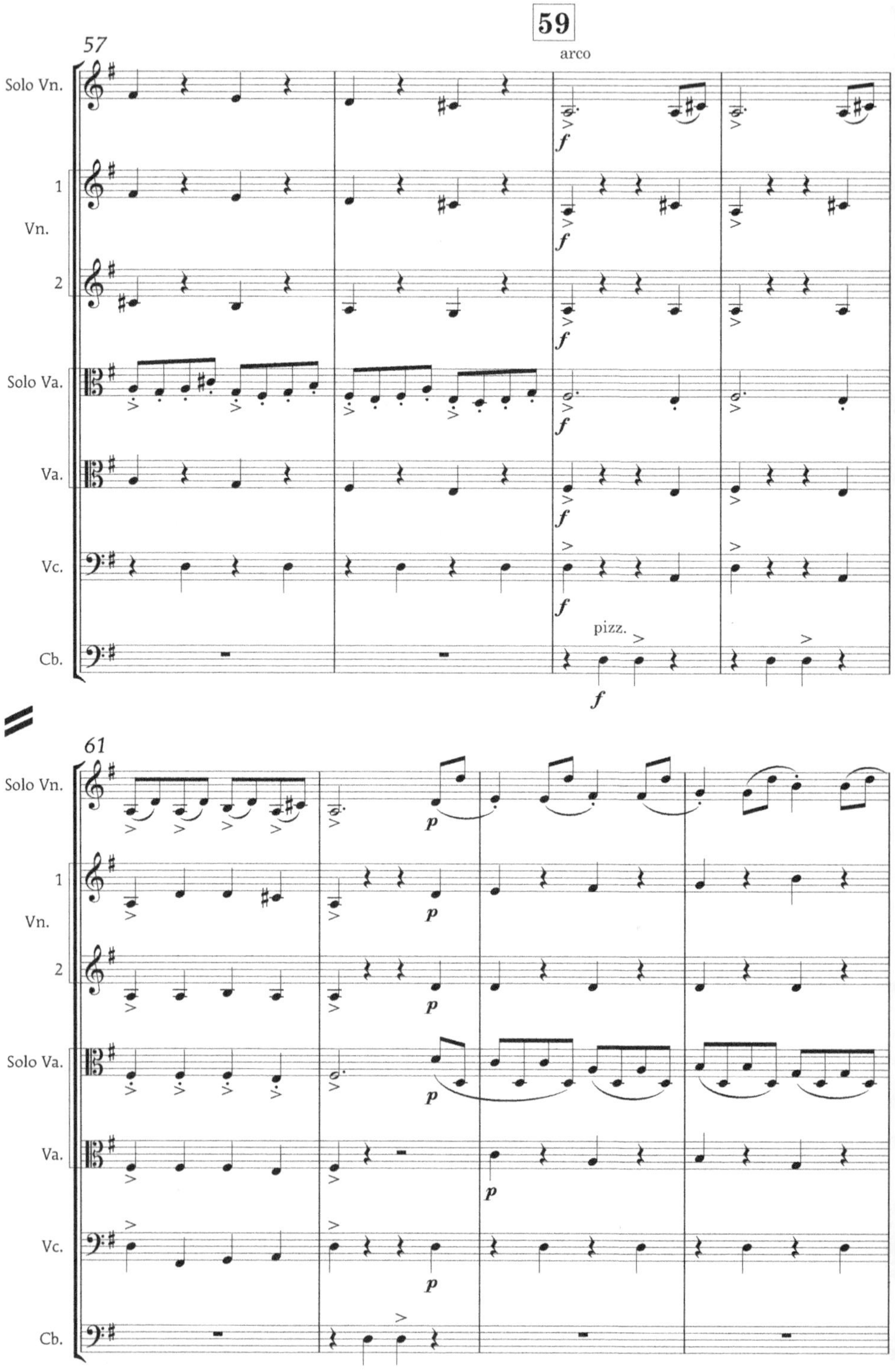
59
57
arco
Solo Vn.
1
Vn.
2
Solo Va.
Va.
Vc.
Cb.
pizz.
61

57

73
Solo Vn.
1
Vn.
2
Solo Va.
Va.
Vc.
arco
ff
Cb.
arco
ff
rit.
a tempo
poco meno mosso
77
ff
unis. arco
ff
unis. arco
ff
ffz
p
arco
ff
ffz

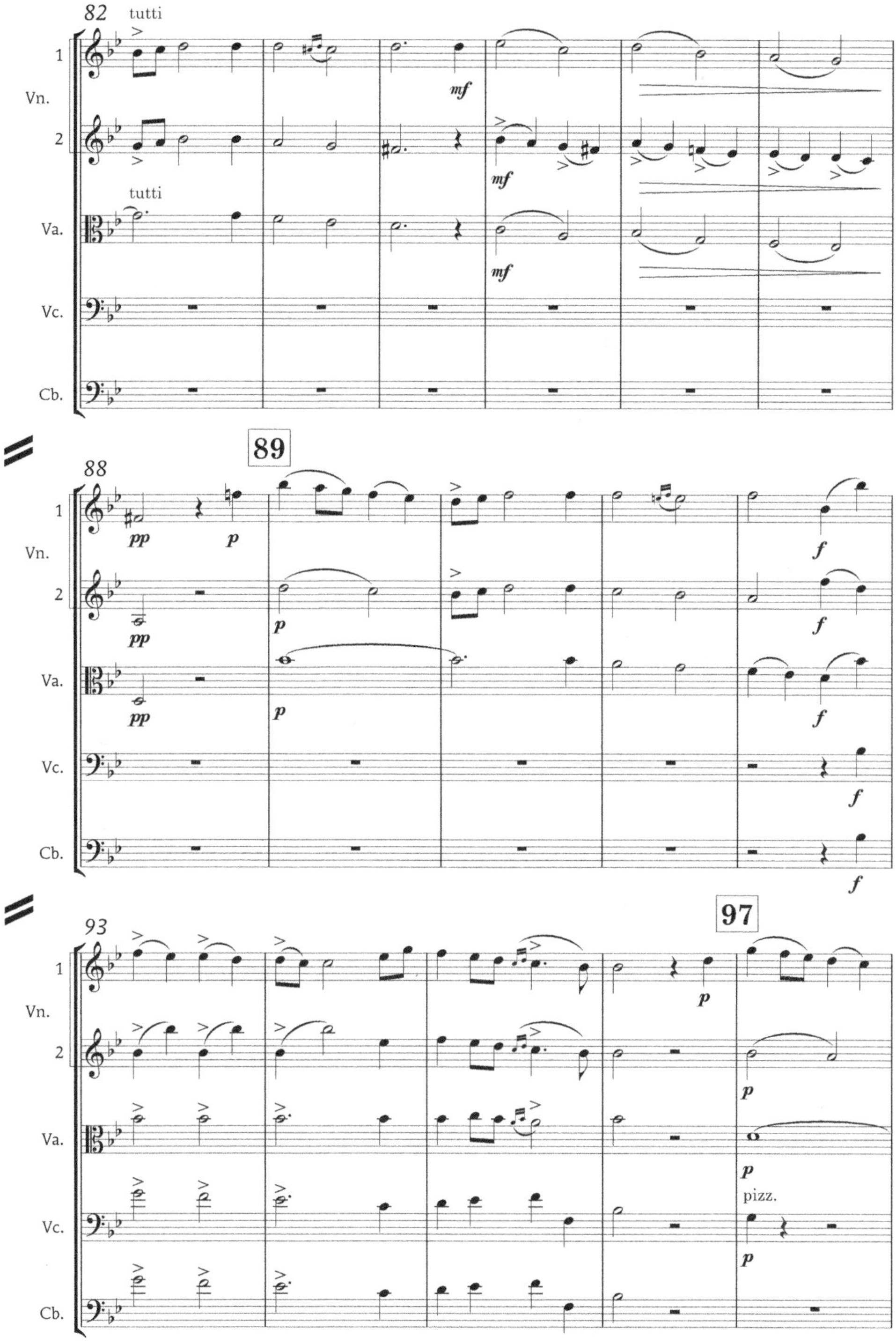
82
tutti
Vn.
1
2
mf
tutti
Va.
mf
Vc.
Cb.
89
88
pp
p
f
97
93
p
pizz.

98
Vn. 1
2
Va.
Vc.
Cb.
arco
pizz.
p
103
cresc.
ff
arco
108
sul G
p più tranq.

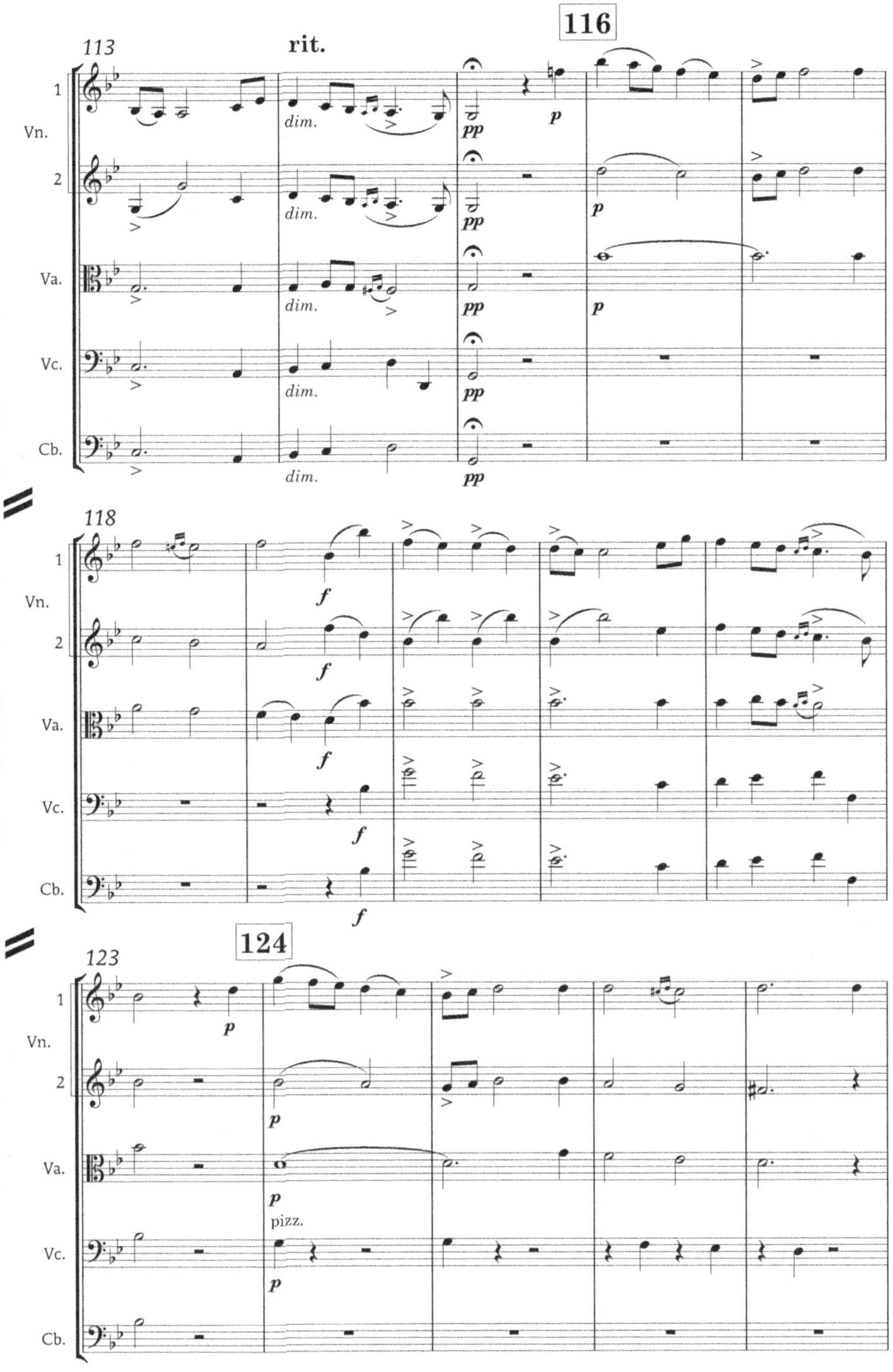
116
113
rit.
Vn. 1 2
Va.
Vc.
Cb.
dim.
pp
p
118
f
124
123
pizz.

128
Vn.
1
2
Va.
Vc.
Cb.
arco
pizz.
p
cresc.
133
ff
arco
138
sul G
p più tranq.
rit.
dim.
pp
solo
spicc.
p

63

151
Solo Vn.
unis.
Vn.
1
p
unis.
2
p
Solo Va.
p
pizz.
Va.
p
Vc.
Cb.
155
Solo Vn.
pizz.
cresc.
Vn.
1
cresc.
2
cresc.
Solo Va.
cresc.
Va.
cresc.
pizz.
Vc.
p
cresc.
Cb.

65

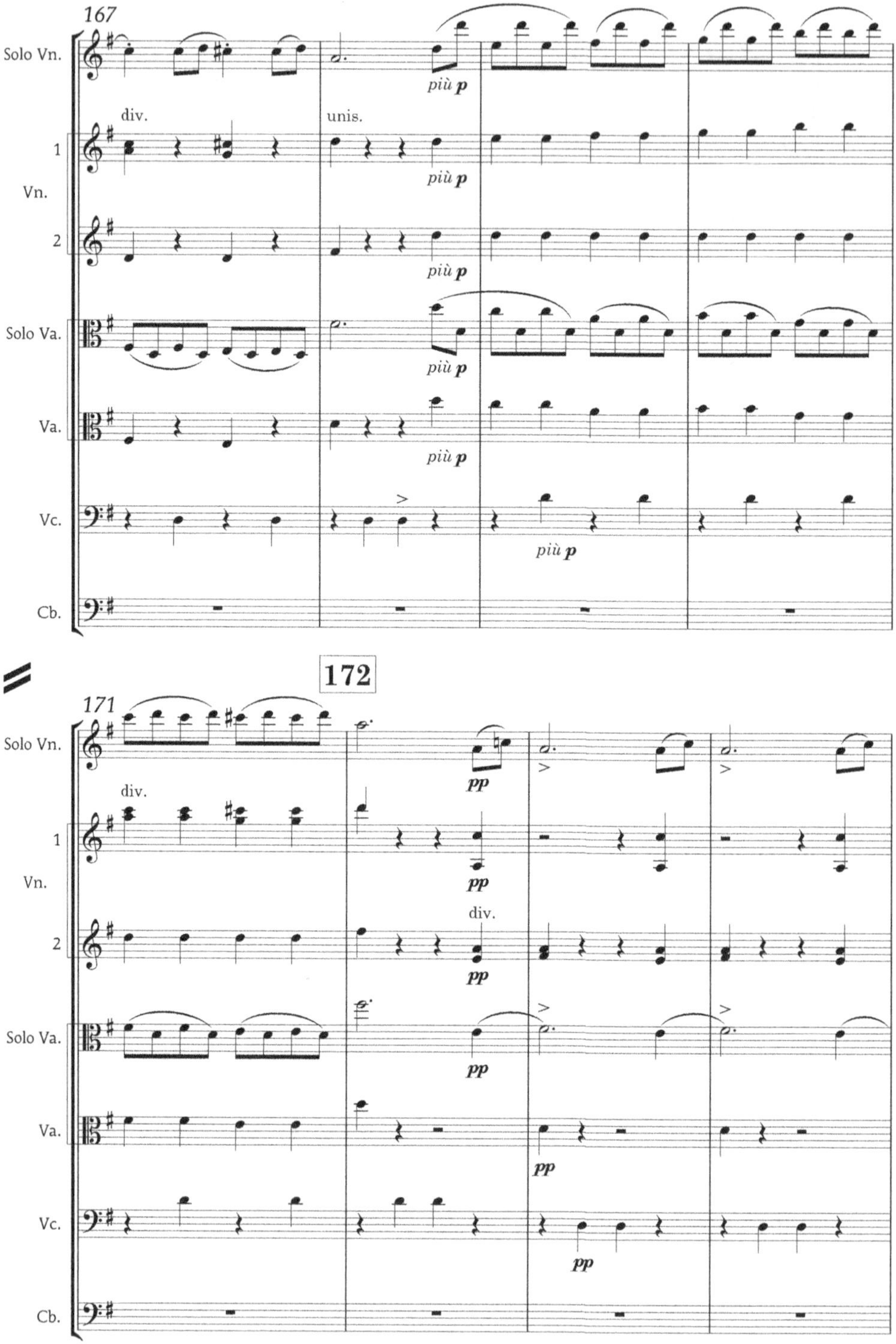
167
Solo Vn.
più p
div.
unis.
1
Vn.
2
Solo Va.
Va.
Vc.
Cb.
172
171
pp

67

Made in the USA
Coppell, TX
12 March 2025

47027726R00042